KS1
4–6
Years

Master Maths at Home

Multiplication, Division and Fractions

Scan the QR code to help your child's learning at home.

  MATHS NO PROBLEM!

mastermathsathome.com

How to use this book

Maths — No Problem! created **Master Maths at Home** to help children develop fluency in the subject and a rich understanding of core concepts.

Key features of the Master Maths at Home books include:

- Carefully designed lessons that provide structure but also allow flexibility in how they're used. For example, some children may want to write numbers, while others might want to trace.

- Speech bubbles containing content designed to spark diverse conversations, with many discussion points that don't have obvious 'right' or 'wrong' answers.

- Rich illustrations that will guide children to a discussion of shapes and units of measurement, allowing them to make connections to the wider world around them.

- Exercises that allow a flexible approach and can be adapted to suit any child's cognitive or functional ability.

- Clearly laid out pages that encourage children to practise a range of higher-order skills.

- A community of friendly and relatable characters who introduce each lesson and come along as your child progresses through the series.

You can see more guidance on how to use these books at **mastermathsathome.com**.

We're excited to share all the ways you can learn maths!

Copyright © 2022 Maths — No Problem!

Maths — No Problem!
mastermathsathome.com
www.mathsnoproblem.com
hello@mathsnoproblem.com

First published in Great Britain in 2022 by
Dorling Kindersley Limited
One Embassy Gardens, 8 Viaduct Gardens, London SW11 7BW
A Penguin Random House Company

The authorised representative in the EEA is Dorling Kindersley
Verlag GmbH. Amulfstr. 124, 80636 Munich, Germany

10 9 8 7 6 5 4 3 2 1
001–327065–Jan/22

A CIP catalogue record for this book is available from the British Library.

ISBN: 978-0-24153-905-7
Printed and bound in China

For the curious
www.dk.com

This book was made with Forest Stewardship Council™ certified paper - one small step in DK's commitment to a sustainable future. For more information go to www.dk.com/our-green-pledge

Acknowledgements
The publisher would like to thank the authors and consultants Andy Psarianos, Judy Hornigold, Adam Gifford and Dr Anne Hermanson.

The Castledown typeface has been used with permission from the Colophon Foundry.

Contents

Ruby   Elliott   Amira   Charles   Lulu   Sam   Oak   Holly   Ravi   Emma   Jacob   Hannah

Equal groups

Starter

Are the 🧁 and the 🍌 in equal groups?

Example

There are
3 bunches of 🍌.

A group of 🍌 is
called a bunch.

Each bunch
has a different number of 🍌.
The groups are not equal.

4

There are 4 boxes of .

Each box has 4 . All the boxes have an equal number of cupcakes.

The 🍌 are not in equal groups.

The 🧁 are in equal groups.

1 Who has made equal groups?
Tick (✓) the correct box.

(a)

(b)

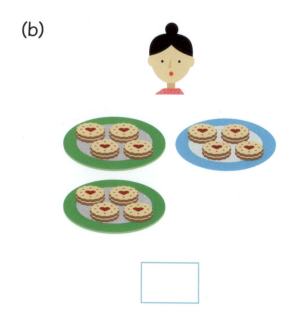

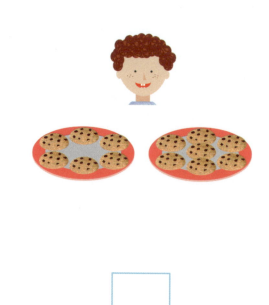

2 Fill in the blanks.

(a)

There are ⬜ equal groups.

Each group has ⬜ drinks.

(b)

There are ⬜ equal groups.

Each group has ⬜ drinks.

Repeated addition

Starter

How many cars are there?
How many children are in each car?
How many children are there in total?

Example

There are 4 cars.

Each car has 2 children in it.

8

Each car has 2 children.
There are 4 groups of 2.

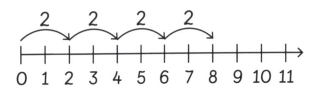

There are 8 children in total.

4 groups of 2 = 8
2 + 2 + 2 + 2 = 8
4 twos = 8

Practice

Fill in the blanks.

1

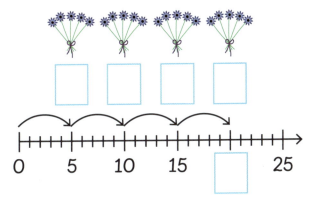

(a) There are ☐ groups.

(b) Each group has ☐ flowers.

2

(a) ☐ groups of ☐ = ☐

(b) There are ☐ crayons in total.

Arrays

Starter

How many carrots are there in the garden bed?

Example

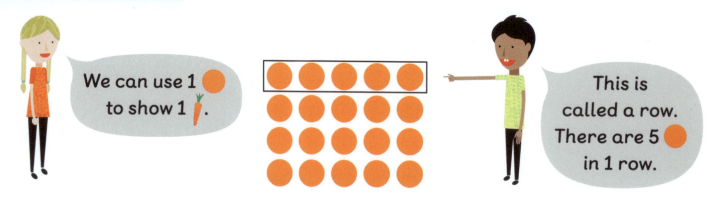

We can use 1 🟠 to show 1 🥕.

This is called a row. There are 5 🟠 in 1 row.

There are 4 rows. Each row has 5 🟠 .

1 row of 5 = 5
2 rows of 5 = 10
3 rows of 5 = 15
4 rows of 5 = 20

There are 20 🥕 in total.

Fill in the blanks.

1 3 rows of 2

There are [ ] rows of 2 .

[ ] twos = [ ]

There are [ ] in total.

2 3 rows of 3 ●

There are [ ] rows of [ ] ● .

[ ] threes = [ ]

There are [ ] ● in total.

3

There are [ ] 🟢 in each row.

There are [ ] rows.

[ ] rows of [ ] = [ ]

There are [ ] 🟢 in total.

4

There are ⬚ rows of .

There are ⬚ rows of .

There is ⬚ row of .

There are ⬚ counters in each row.

There are ⬚ rows in total.

⬚ rows of ⬚ = ⬚

There are ⬚ counters in total.

5   ⬚ rows of ⬚ = ⬚

6 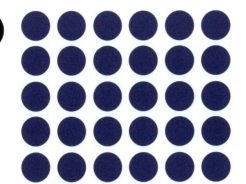 ☐ rows of ☐ = ☐

7 Fill in the blanks and draw lines to match.

5 rows of 3 = ☐ •

•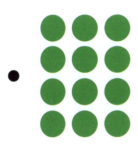

2 rows of 6 = ☐ •

•

4 rows of 3 = ☐ •

•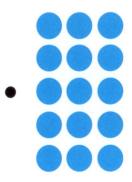

3 rows of 5 = ☐ •

•

13

Doubles

Starter

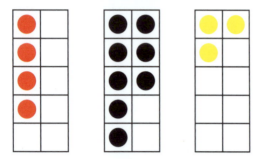

Can you double these numbers?

Example

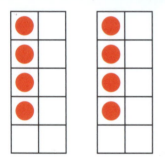

Double 4 = 8

Double 4 means
2 fours.

2 eights is
equal to 16.

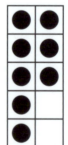 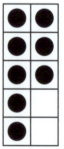

Double 8 = 16

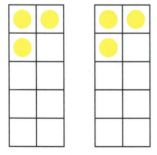

2 threes is equal to 6.

Double 3 = 6

Fill in the blanks.

1

Double ☐

= ☐

Double ☐

= ☐

Double ☐

= ☐

Double ☐

= ☐

Double ☐

= ☐

Double ☐

= ☐

Double ☐

= ☐

Double ☐

= ☐

Double ☐

= ☐

Double ☐

= ☐

Page 23   (d) 2 **3** There are 4 ways: groups of 2, 3, 4 and 6.

Page 25   **1** There are 12 toy robots in total. There are 4 boxes. There are 3 in each box.

Page 26   **2** There are 4 doughnuts in each group. **3** There are 6 apples in total. There are 3 plates. Each plate has 2 apples.

Page 27   **4** There are 3 mangoes in each box.

Page 29   **1 (a)**   **(b)**

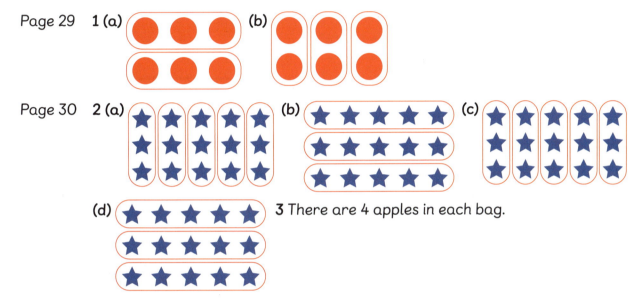

Page 30   **2 (a)**   **(b)**   **(c)**

(d)   **3** There are 4 apples in each bag.

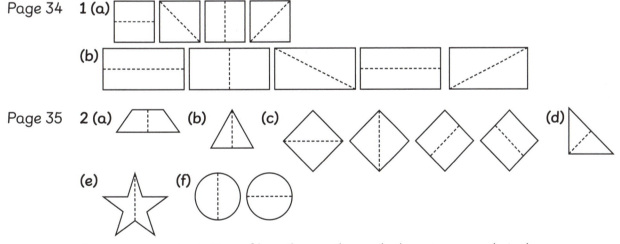

Page 31   **4** 5 plates **5** There are 9 flowers in total. There are 3 vases. There are 3 flowers in each vase.

Page 34   **1 (a)**

(b)

Page 35   **2 (a)**   **(b)**   **(c)**   **(d)**

(e)   **(f)**

Accept any orientation of line drawn through the square and circle.

Page 37   **1 1** part of the shape shaded. For example:

(a)   **(b)**   **(c)**   **(d)**

Page 38   **2 (b)** ✓ **(c)** ✓ **(e)** ✓ **(f)** ✓

Answers continued

Page 39   **3** 2 biscuits **4** 4 chocolates **5** 1 quarter of 12 doughnuts is 3 doughnuts.

Page 40   **1 (a)** ✓ **2** There are 5 equal groups. There are 5 in each group.

Page 41   **3** 5, 10, 20. There are 4 groups. Each group has 5 flowers. **4** There are 3 counters in each row. There are 5 rows. 5 rows of 3 = 15. There are 15 counters.

Page 42   **5** There are 5 counters in each row. There are 3 rows. 3 rows of 5 = 15. There are 15 counters. **6 (a)** double 4 = 8 **(b)** double 10 = 20.

Page 43   **7** Ruby has 15 flowers, and Sam has 12 flowers, Ruby has more **8 (a)** There are 5 groups of 2 drinks **(b)** There are 4 groups of 10 ice creams.

Page 44   **9** Each plate has 3 pears. **10** Each plate should have 5 grapes.

Page 45   **11**

12

13 5 cookies go on the plate.